the underwater world of

The
Coral Reef

by ANN McGOVERN

FOUR WINDS PRESS   NEW YORK

For Marty

*my all-time diving buddy
and for my favorite Christmas
diving buddies:*

Jim, Annie, Charles, and Peter

PHOTO CREDITS

S. C. Bisserot/Bruce Coleman, Inc.: 24, 25; Jane Burton/Bruce Coleman, Inc.: 17; Dick Clarke: cover; Joan Farber: 16; Peter McGovern: 22; Tom McHugh/Photo Researchers, Inc.: 29; Allan Power/Bruce Coleman, Inc.: 10, 11, 18, 19, 21; Martin L. Scheiner: 6, 8, 12, 14, 15, 16, 23, 26, 27, 30, 31, 32, 33, 35, 37.

323

LIBRARY OF CONGRESS CATALOGING IN PUBLICATION DATA

McGovern, Ann.
    The underwater world of the coral reef.

    Includes index.
    SUMMARY: Describes the building of coral reefs and
the animal life going on around them.
    1. Coral reef biology—Juvenile literature.
[1. Coral reef biology.   2.   Marine biology]   I.   Title.

QH95.8.M3   574.92   75–44305
ISBN 0–590–07467–9

Published by Four Winds Press
A Division of Scholastic Magazines, Inc., New York, N.Y.
Copyright © 1976 by Ann McGovern

1   2   3   4   5   80   79   78   77   76

Contents

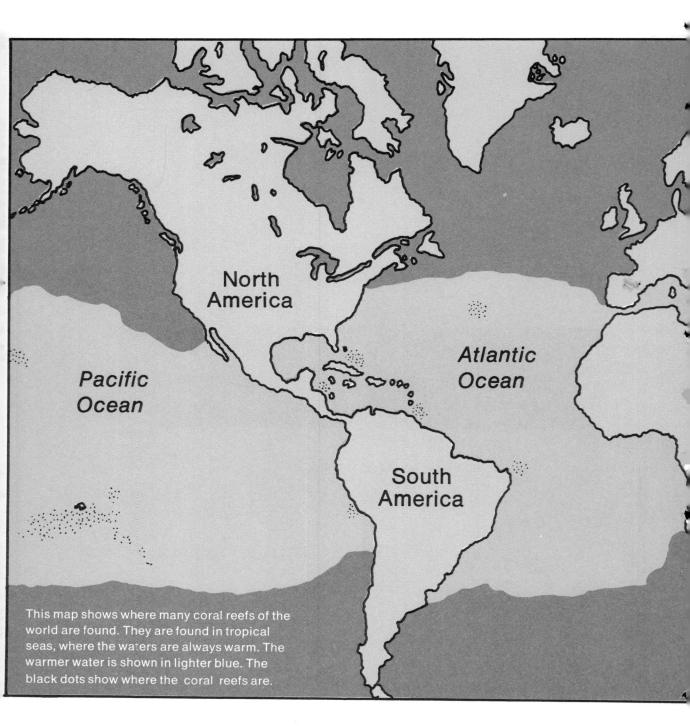

North
America

Pacific
Ocean

Atlantic
Ocean

South
America

This map shows where many coral reefs of the world are found. They are found in tropical seas, where the waters are always warm. The warmer water is shown in lighter blue. The black dots show where the coral reefs are.

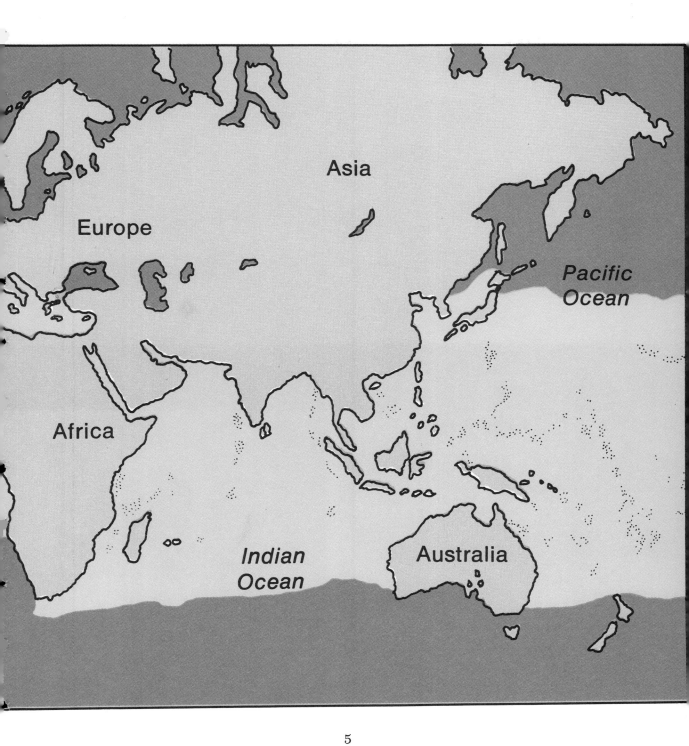

Asia

Europe

Pacific
Ocean

Africa

Indian
Ocean

Australia

A Magic Place Beneath the Sea

There is a strange and beautiful place beneath the sea. It is a place of towers and tunnels, caves and castles.

Red trees and green mushrooms grow on steep cliffs in the water.

Purple lacy fans sway gently to and fro.

The water is alive with creatures in all the colors of the rainbow. Some have stripes. Others have dots. A few are as big as pillows. Others are smaller than your thumb.

A pink basket behind a rock is so big you could hide in it. A white Christmas tree the size of a penny grows on another rock.

Blue fingers reach up toward the top of the sea. A forest of horns and spiky antlers grows nearby.

It looks like a fairyland.
But it is a real place.
It is a coral reef beneath the sea.

Where Can You Find a Coral Reef?

There are coral reefs in clear warm waters beneath the sea in many of the warm places of the world.

Coral reefs need light and warmth from the sun. The sun's light can reach down only about 300 feet in clear water — about as far as a rope hanging down from a 30-story building.

The sea floor is very uneven. When the sea floor is deeper than 300 feet, no coral reef can grow.

Coral reefs grow upward from the sandy sea floor. They grow toward the top of the warm waters.

Morning on a Reef

It is morning on a coral reef. The sun warms the water and lights up the reef below.

The color of the reef is mostly a soft blue-green. But there are flashes of bright colors everywhere — colors of fish and of the many other creatures that live here.

A purple fish with blue dots swims out of a hole in the coral wall.

A big red crab hides beneath a ledge.

A green eel stretches its head out of a cave.

Dozens of blue fish with yellow stripes dart this way and that.

The fish swim over purple sponges and over coral rocks splashed with color. The corals look like dozens of tiny rock flowers and rock stars.

The fish, the crab, the eels are all animals you can see. But there are billions more you don't see. Some of the *polyps* (say PA-LIPS) — little animals that build a coral reef — are too small to see.

Tube coral with polyps feeding   Tube coral with polyps inside

The Building of a Coral Reef

Dozens of different kinds of hard stony coral grow on a reef. Each kind of coral has a special shape. Some look like castles and cliffs. Some look like mushrooms or stars or brains. Some look like animal horns or lettuce leaves.

All these differently shaped hard corals were made by the little polyp animals. Some polyps are as tiny as a grain of sand. Some are as large as your hand.

A kind of limestone oozes out of each soft little polyp and forms a stony cup around it. The polyp is attached to the inside of the cup. It can stretch out to eat but it can never leave the cup to swim away.

Millions and millions of these coral cups join together to form the hard coral shapes on the reef.

When the polyps die, new coral polyps build their cups on top of the cups of the dead polyps.

And so the reef grows — growing slowly, growing bigger and wider.

It takes millions of years, but these little polyps can build a coral reef hundreds of miles long, like the Great Barrier Reef in Australia.

As you are reading this page, at this very moment, new reefs are silently growing in the warm blue-green waters of the tropical seas.

Vase sponge

Magic Gardens in the Sea

Soft branches sway in the clear water. Sea plumes and sea whips look like plants from a magic garden.

But they aren't plants. They are polyps. The soft corals are made of billions of little polyps joined together. These polyps don't make stony cups like the hard coral polyps.

Other animals on the reef look like flowers and fans. A feathery "flower" grows on a coral cliff. A big fish swims close to it. Poof.

The feathery flower disappears, shooting back into its tubelike shell. This feathery "flower" is really an animal — a plume worm. Guess who its cousins are? Common earthworms.

Other beautiful animals are the sea anemones (AN-NEM-O-NEES). Their long swaying tubes are covered with stingers which they use to kill their food.

A little fish swims over a tube sponge. Sponges are animals too. They grow in shapes that sometimes look like vases and fingers and barrels.

Tube sponge

Spiny lobster

Starfish

Who Lives on the Reef?

It is the middle of the day.

In holes, inside coral caves, and under coral ledges, fish are swimming or resting or eating.

Fish are everywhere.

There are fish eating on the white sandy bottom. There are fish swimming over the grasses, just beyond the reef.

Fish peep out of tall sponges. Fish swim in and around the many corals of the reef.

Other creatures also make their home on the coral reef. Huge crabs, starfish, tiny shrimp, and spiny lobsters live here too.

From time to time, turtles and sharks come by, but the reef is not their real home. They live in the deeper waters of the open sea.

Feeding Time

At this very moment, there are millions of fish gobbling food.

On a coral reef, feeding time is all the time. It never stops. Some creatures hunt for food at night. But most fish find their food by day.

What are they eating? Everything from tiny *plankton* — the smallest plants and animals that drift through the water — to big fish.

Sometimes you can tell what kind of food a fish eats by the size of its mouth.

Most fish with small mouths eat plankton.

Most fish with big mouths and sharp teeth eat other fish.

The *longnose butterfly fish* pokes into tiny cracks and holes in the coral for its food. Its mouth is at the end of its long nose.

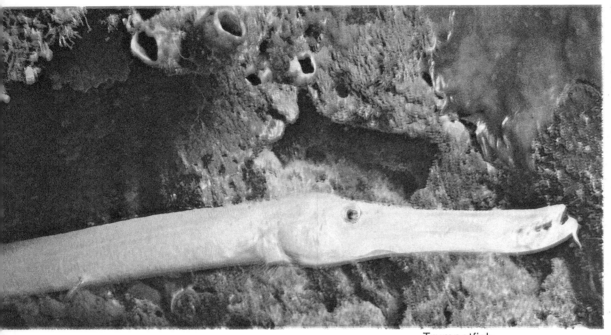
Trumpetfish

With its strawlike mouth the *trumpetfish* sucks in its food.

Whiskers on its chin help the *goatfish* find its food on the sandy bottom.

The *trunkfish* can blow jets of water over the sand to uncover its food.

Here comes a four-foot *grouper* with a huge mouth. A young grouper feeds on tiny shrimp. But when it gets older, it can swallow a fish one foot long in one gulp.

It's easy to see why the *spiny sea urchin* is called the pincushion of the sea. Long spiny needles stick out all over its body.

It's not so easy to see why any fish would want to eat one. But hungry sharks eat the whole thing.

Some fish will eat members of their own family.

And some fish even find their meals on the backs of other fish.

A Cleaning Station on a Reef

Two tiny yellow fish dart over the round brain coral. A big blue fish swims slowly above it.

Suddenly the blue fish stops swimming. It points its head down toward the brain coral and stays perfectly still.

This is a signal for the yellow fish. They leave the brain coral and swim up, right onto the back of the blue fish. The blue fish is about 10 times as big as the yellow fish.

The yellow fish pick at and nip off tiny animals, the *parasites* that grow on the skins of the big fish. The yellow fish eat these parasites.

In a few seconds, the blue fish gives itself a little shake, points its head up and swims away — nice and clean. The two yellow fish go back to the brain coral where they wait for the next big fish to come along.

The brain coral is a "cleaning station." The two yellow fish — *gobies* — are fish-cleaning fish.

A fish-cleaning
fish at work on
a big fish

There are many cleaning stations on a coral reef. And there are many fish busy picking off the parasites that grow on bigger fish.

Sometimes a cleaning station gets very busy. Sometimes fish have to wait their turn to get cleaned.

Some fish only work as fish-cleaning fish when they are young and small. When they grow up and get bigger, they need to eat bigger food.

The little fish-cleaning fish are always safe when they are cleaning big fish. Very big fish won't eat the little fish that are cleaning them, even when the little fish go after parasites in a big fish's mouth.

Foureye butterfly fish

Danger!

An enemy is near. A big fish is after a *foureye butterfly fish*. But the big fish can't tell if the butterfly fish is coming or going. The foureye butterfly fish can fool its enemies with the two round black spots on its back that look like eyes. The butterfly fish is safe — this time.

There is always danger on a coral reef. Fish must eat to live. And many big fish eat other creatures.

How do fish protect themselves from danger?

There are good hiding places all over the reef. Some fish live in tiny places where bigger fish can't fit.

Some fish dig up the sand with their fins, making holes to hide in.

Some fish have spines. These are useful in times of danger. *Blue tangs* have spines near their fins. *Sting rays* have one or two spines on their tails. *Porcupine fish* are covered with spines.

Some fish have streamlined bodies that are built for speed. They can swim away from their enemies in a flash.

An *octopus* shoots out a cloud of black ink. For a moment the ink blinds the octopus's enemy, giving the octopus time to swim to safety.

A group of fish swim by. When one turns, all the fish turn. They swim close together. The group of fish is called a *school*. Fish in schools are safer than fish swimming alone. Why? A hungry enemy often gets confused and doesn't know which fish to go after.

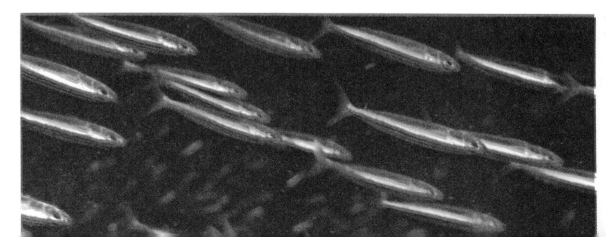

Blue angelfish

Color on the Reef

In the branches of brown coral, a long slender brown trumpetfish is hiding. It swims out of its brown hiding place and its color changes from brown to yellow.

Other reef creatures can change their colors too, when they swim to different places. But some stay the same color as their background.

A *stone fish* looks just like a rock. A *lizardfish* blends in with the sandy bottom.

But some fish of the reef have colors that glow like jewels.

Why are these fish so colorful? Scientists say there are different reasons.

Queen angelfish

Every fish has its own special place on the reef where it lives. So color may be the signal for other fish to stay away.

But color can also attract. Fish look for members of their own families at mating time.

Color may also be important to the fish that swim in schools. If by chance a fish gets separated from the others, their color may help guide it back to its school.

Many fish go through a color change when they get older. Some have stripes or dots when they are young but these markings disappear as they grow older.

This young yellow fish is a blue tang, yet
the only part of it that's blue is the color
around its eyes. When it grows up, it will
turn all blue without a bit of yellow.

Some sea creatures change color when
they are excited or frightened. The octopus
can go from white to deep red in a few
seconds.

Some fish change color when the light on
the reef changes.

Giants on the Reef

It is late afternoon. The sun is low in the sky. The sun's light is dim in the waters of the coral reef.

The silver *barracuda* is hungry. It darts after a fish. Its long body is built for speed. Its many teeth are sharp. Snap! The fish has become another meal for the barracuda.

A large shadow glides over the sand. It is a *spotted eagle ray.* It seems to fly like a huge bird, but its wide "wings" are special fins that ripple as it glides. Some rays have sawlike spines on their whiplike tails.

The shark rests on the bottom of the reef. Its head is inside a coral cave. It is a small shark, as sharks go — about three feet long. It is a *nurse shark,* one of the many harmless sharks of the sea. Bigger sharks live in deeper waters and hardly ever come to the coral reef.

A long green *moray eel* looks like a giant snake. It lives in caves. The moray eel sticks its head out of the cave in the daytime, but waits until night to swim over the reef for food.

One of the biggest fish in the sea is a giant sea bass called a *jewfish.* It can grow to be twice as long as you, and it can weigh over 600 pounds.

Night on the Reef

It is night on the coral reef. The waters are as dark as the night sky.

Some nights when the moon is full, a silver light glows on the reef.

Nighttime is the time for some of the corals of the reef to eat. By day these coral polyps hide. Each polyp has a slit for a mouth and tentacles that reach out to trap food.

The reef is alive at night with creatures that were hiding or asleep in the daytime.

Other creatures who were awake in the daytime are sleeping now.

Fish have no eyelids. They sleep with their eyes open!

Some fish sleep in holes or cracks. Others bury themselves in the sand. *Parrotfish* spin a kind of cocoon around themselves at night.

Some fish change their color at night. The bright blue tangs become striped. Yellow and blue fish turn gray. Even some bright red *squirrelfish* become paler. These color changes help hide the fish from the enemies of the night.

Squirrelfish

Moray eels slither out of their caves and glide like snakes across the dark sand.

Lobsters, crabs, and delicate shrimp move about freely in the darkness. The octopus comes out of hiding to feed on crabs.

The spiny sea urchins move slowly down the walls of the reef and across the sandy bottom, looking like walking pin cushions.

By day the *basket starfish* looks like tangled thread. But at night the "threads" become lacy arms, reaching out for a meal of plankton.

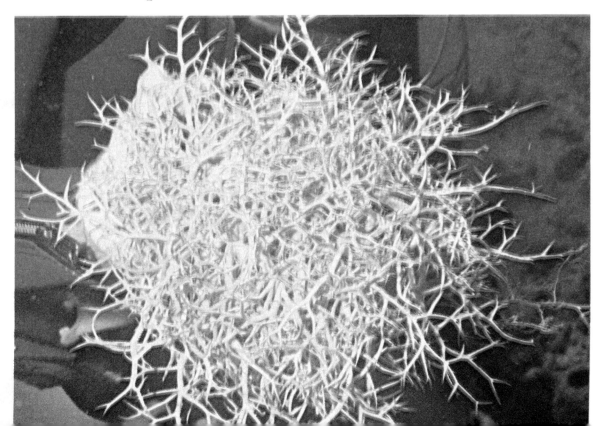

Strange Visitors

The first light of day shines on the coral reef. The night creatures return to their hiding places to wait for darkness. The day creatures awake and begin to look for food.

Later the sun is bright in the sky and lights up the reef below.

A long shadow appears at the top of the water — the shadow of a boat.

Splash. Strange forms begin swimming down — down from the top of the water all the way to the reef below.

The strange forms are people. On their backs are tanks of air. They are scuba divers. They breathe in air through a regulator and blow out big bubbles that shine in the clear sunlit waters.

Divers are weightless in the water. They are as light and as free as any fish in the sea.

They can turn somersaults. Or stand on their heads. Or sit quietly on the sandy bottom and watch the fish. Or soar gently over a garden of coral. Or float slowly down the sides of a steep cliff.

With just a glass face mask and a breathing tube called a *snorkel,* people can float on the top of the water and look down at the wonders of the reef below.

But scuba divers can dive deep. They often dive down 100 feet or more. That's like going off the top of a 10-story building.

Thousands of people go scuba diving just for fun. Others dive to take pictures (like the pictures in this book) with special underwater cameras.

Some people search for treasure in the sea or explore a ship that sank long ago.

Scientists go scuba diving to study the life on the coral reef.

Maybe someday you will dive down to a coral reef in the sea. Then you can discover for yourself the many wonders of this magic world.

The Magic Goes On and On

New corals grow slowly.

New creatures are born in the water.

Small creatures find their food on the reef.
They themselves become food for larger
creatures.

Life on the coral reef is always growing
and changing.

Night and day.

Day and night.

Right now.

Index

A page number printed in heavy type means there is a picture on that page.

Acknowledgment

The author acknowledges with thanks
the invaluable assistance given by Dr. C.L. Smith
of The American Museum of Natural History.

Thanks, too to the Baskin family who
turned us into joyful scuba divers, to
Bert and Jackie Kilbride, Virgin Gorda,
B.W.I., whose love of the underwater
world is infectious, and to the
wonderful people at Little Dix Bay,
Virgin Gorda, B.W.I.